Color America's National Parks

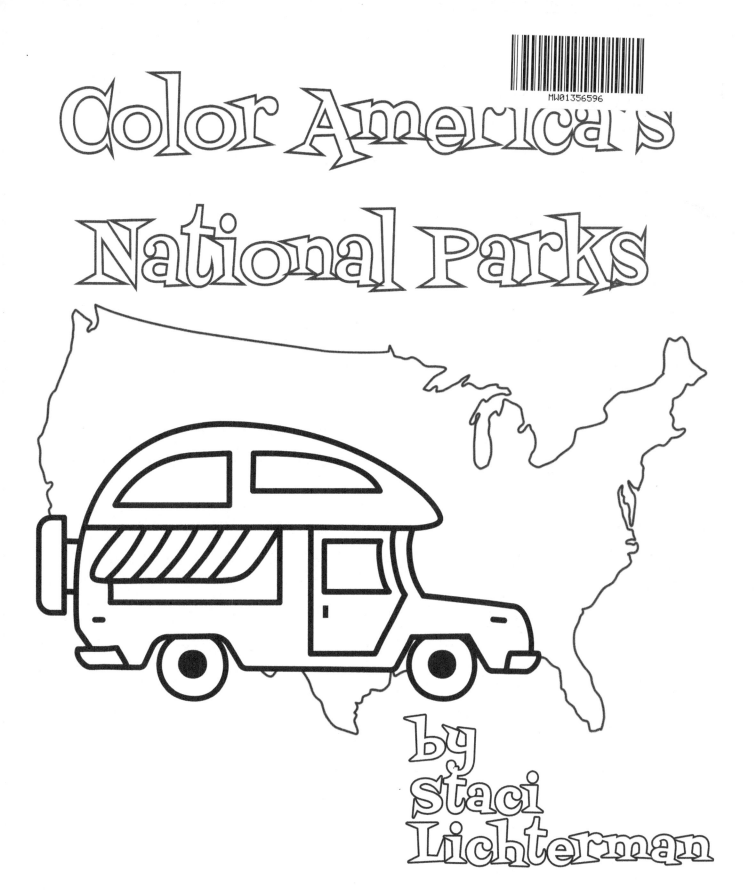

by Staci Lichterman

This coloring book celebrates several of America's National Parks. The pages were adapted from the archive of WPA Posters available from the Library of Congress.

The WPA National Park Posters project took place after The Dustbowl Years but before World War II. The thirteen original posters created between 1938 and 1941 are some of the most iconic advertisements from the era.

For many years the posters were forgotten. However, they were rediscovered by a park ranger named David Lean in the 1970s & continue to be popular today. This book celebrates the natural wonders found in the US National Park system as well as the art inspired by them.

Enjoy exploring!

Staci

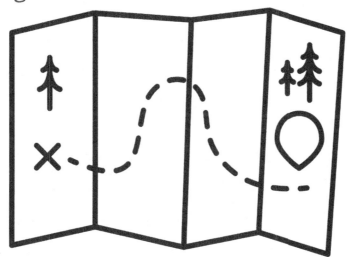

Park Pages

- [ ] Acadia National Park, Maine
- [ ] Horseshoe Bend, Arizona
- [ ] Bryce Canyon National Park, Utah
- [ ] Canyonlands National Park, Utah
- [ ] Capitol Reef National Park, Utah
- [ ] Zion National Park, Utah
- [ ] Arches National Park, Utah
- [ ] Crater Lake National Park, Oregon
- [ ] Death Valley National Park, California
- [ ] Yosemite National Park, California
- [ ] Glacier National Park, Montana
- [ ] Volcano National Park, Hawaii
- [ ] Petrified Forest National Park, Arizona
- [ ] Old Faithful, Yellowstone National Park, Wyoming
- [ ] Joshua Tree National Park, California
- [ ] Saguaro National Park, Arizona
- [ ] Grand Canyon National Park, Arizona
- [ ] Isle Royale National Park, Michigan
- [ ] New River Gorge National Park, West Virginia
- [ ] Grand Teton National Park, Wyoming
- [ ] Mount Rainier National Park, Washington
- [ ] Carlsbad Caverns National Park, New Mexico

Color Testing Page

Horseshoe Bend

Bryce Canyon National Park

Crater Lake National Park

Crater Lake National Park is in Oregon's Cascade Mountains. It's known for its namesake Crater Lake, the deepest lake in the United States. Theodore Roosevelt established Crater Lake as a national park in 1902.

Death

Valley

Glacier National Park

Glacier National Park is named for the remnants of ice age glaciers. It is located in Montana and borders Waterton Lakes National Park in Alberta, Canada. The pair are called the "Crown of the Continent," because of the huge variety of natural beauty.

When Glacier Park became a national park in 1910, it had 35 glaciers. Due to global warming there were less than 25 left in 2020.

Future Ranger

Mmm S'mores

Joshua Tree

The Grand Canyon

Isle Royale

Isle Royale National Park, located in the waters of Lake Superior, is America's **least** visited national park. In fact, there is no way to drive to Isle Royale. You need to fly or take a boat from Michigan, Minnesota or Ontario, Canada to visit.

America's newest national park is **New River Gorge National Park**, located in West Virginia. It is the 63rd national park and the first created by President Joe Biden. New River Gorge Bridge is the most iconic site in the new park, known for hiking, fishing and miles of Class III-IV whitewater rapids.

Hot Springs National Park in Hot Springs, Arkansas is the first land in America to be protected as national federal lands, making it the first (unofficial) national park in **1832**. Before becoming part of the United States as part of The Louisiana Purchase, Hot Springs was considered a sacred, natural wonder among Native Americans.

Hot Springs National Park

Carlsbad Caverns

Carlsbad Caverns National Park is in the Guadalupe Mountains in southern New Mexico. It features more than 100 caves. Walking from the Natural Entrance to the largest cave, the "Big Room" is like walking down a **75** story building. It is well worth the hour walk to see some of the craziest, most beautiful rock formations called stalactites and stalagmites.

What Park Should We Visit Next?

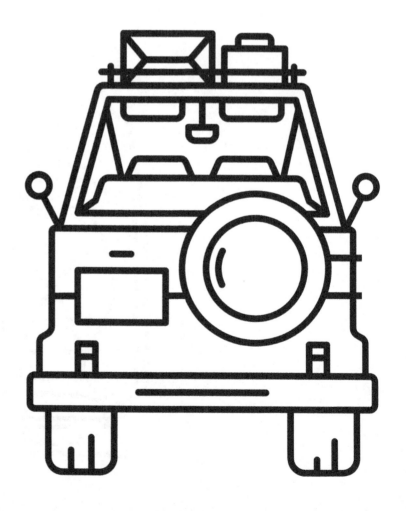

My Bucket List

Parks I've Visited

Color Testing Page

Made in the USA
Middletown, DE
23 April 2023